WISING UP

WISING UP

How I Mastered the Rinse Cycle and Other Lessons of Life

William G. Johnsson

REVIEW AND HERALD® PUBLISHING ASSOCIATION
HAGERSTOWN, MD 21740

The author assumes full responsibility for the accuracy of all facts and quotations as cited in this book.

This book was
Edited by Richard W. Coffen
Designed by Bill Kirstein
Cover photo by Dennis Crews
Typeset: 11.5/13 Korinna

Texts credited to NIV are from the *Holy Bible, New International Version*. Copyright © 1973, 1978, International Bible Society. Used by permission of Zondervan Bible Publishers.

PRINTED IN U.S.A.

96 95 94 93 92   10 9 8 7 6 5 4 3 2

Library of Congress Cataloging in Publication Data
Johnsson, William G., 1934-
    Wising Up : how I mastered the rinse cycle and other lessons of life / William G. Johnsson.
        p. cm.
    1. Meditations. 2. Johnsson, William G., 1934-   . I. Title.
BV4832.2.J619 1991
242—dc20   91-35753
                                                             CIP
ISBN 0-8280-0637-7

Father Labat's Discount Book of the Dead

Poems by T.A. Haverkamp

Kansas City Spartan Press Missouri

Spartan Press

Kansas City, Missouri

spartanpresskc.com

Spartan
Press

Copyright (c) Thad Haverkamp 2017

First Edition 1 3 5 7 9 10 8 6 4 2

ISBN: 978-1-946642-14-1

LCCN: 2017938107

Design, edits and layout: Jason Ryberg

Cover photo and author photos: Atomic Photography

ACKNOWLEDGMENTS

Prospero's Books and Spartan Press would like to thank
Jeanette Powers, j.d.tulloch, Jason Preu, M. Scott
Douglass, Shawn Pavey, Shawn Saving, Jesse Kates,
Jim Holroyd, Steven H.Bridgens, Thomas Mason,
Beth Dille, Mason Wolf, The West Plaza Tomato Co.,
Mark Mclane, the Osage Arts Community and
The Robert J. Deuser Foundation For Libertarian Studies.

Thanks to Jason Ryberg, Mark Hennessy and Maggie
Allen for reminding me why we continue to torture
ourselves on the altar of that wicked goddess —
the Blank Page. And — more thanks than I am capable
of giving — to Danielle Sullivan for both putting up
with me for far too long and being willing to read
and reread every little scribble I jot down.

CONTENTS

To Reed and all of my many friends
on the Other Side.

A Friend on the Other Side

They told me that the old hotel was haunted.

I didn't believe them,
not at first.

Not until I stumbled from the lounge
and lurched my way down the steps into the
dark and empty basement,
looking for the pisser.

The ghost tapped me on the shoulder as I was
standing at the urinal and said,
Boo!

I finished,
gave it a shake,
zipped up
and turned around.

He looked young
and skinny,
his dark hair center-parted and brilliantine shiny,
dressed in a suit
and looking like some junior banker from
back in the day.

And he was translucent.

He said,
Boo.

I smiled, politely,
gave him the *'sup* nod,
and went to wash my hands.

But he wouldn't give up.
He stepped into the reflection
of the men's room mirror,
his face half obscuring mine,
like some cheap, spook-house hologram.

And again he said,
Boo?

I said that I had heard him the first time.

He just stared at me,
like an actor lost on stage,
like he had given me my cue
and now it was my turn
to deliver my lines.

I smiled again and dried my hands on a paper towel.

Finally,
a little sadly,
he said,
So. . .What?. . .Ya' scared?

I told him no.
I said why should I be.

I told him that I had a friend on the other side.
He asked me his name and I told him.

He said that he knew him,
that friend of mine.
Worked a couple of night-shifts with him down
at the boneyard.
Said he seemed like a nice enough guy,
though he really didn't know him all that well.

And I started to feel bad for this button-down,
see-through boy.
I didn't want him to think that he was losing his
touch at the whole specter game.

So I promised him that,
back in the bar,
I would tell all of my friends that I had seen him.
That it was *terrifying*,
That I was *scared shitless*,

You know, out of professional courtesy.

He smiled,
thanked me,
gave the *catch ya' later* nod,
and vanished in an ectoplasmic *pop*.

And I went upstairs,
and told all of my friends
about the ghost that I had seen.
Told them that it was *terrifying*.
Told them that I was *scared shitless*.

But I wasn't,

I mean, why would I be afraid of the ghost of
some kid with greasy hair
in a seersucker suit
when I already have a friend on the other side?

Father Labat's Discount Book of the Dead

Father Labat is at it again,
on the corner of 9th
with his box of books and his one bad eye.

Your name is in here,
and yours,
and your name too!

Father Labat yells at cars.
Father Labat yells at buildings.
Father Labat yells at God.

Father Labat flicks something unseen
from the front of his tattered, black cassock.
He straightens the battered baseball cap on his head.

Funerary rites,
Prophesy
and a roast beef recipe
guaranteed to impress your whole family!

He's got his Bible,
his Holiest of Holies
and his Hosannas on High.

He's got a scratch on his mirrored,
state-trooper-shades,

something crusted in his beard,
a kitten on a leash
and a jug of sacramental wine.

Father Labat can feel a warm wind
rising off the slushy, city street.

He can hear drums.
He can smell rum
and cigars.
He can hear screams.
He has made some Bad Decisions.

Father Labat wanted to die.

But they kicked him back to work off his debt.
They gave him another chance.
They made him a saint.

Father Labat points to his box.
$1 APIECE OR SIX FOR A BUCK,
it says in ragged, Sharpee-black.

Father Labat is trucking in wisdom.
Father Labat is trafficking in glory.
Father Labat is selling the books of the dead.

Sulphur and Nine Pins

I had a bottle of graveyard dirt.

I bought it from my brother
for one pack of cigarettes,
two ounces of whiskey
and a Mercury dime.
Just like the old woman said.

> She told me to wear the dirt in my shoes,
> mixed with salt and red pepper,
> to ward off the most evil of jinxes.

I set the pack on the base of the stone.

> She told me to add it to ginger root
> to attract the love of my dreams.

I put the glass at the foot of the grave
and stepped over it,
backwards,
three times.

> She told me that,
> when mixed with snake-sheds
> and sulfur,
> nine needles and nine pins,
> I could use it to take a life.

I dug up the dirt
and stuck the dime in the hole.

When I was done my knees were stained green,
like when we were boys.
My fingers were dirty.

> She said I could use it
> to do whatever I willed.
> She said it made a powerful hand.

But it couldn't give him back to me.
So I emptied the bottle and gave the dirt back to him.

I dug up the old dime and put it in my pocket.

I drank the whiskey.

I rested against the cold stone monument
and smoked one of the cigarettes.

> I don't care what the old woman said.

I left with deep, dirty stains on my knees
and soft earth on my fingers,
just like when we were boys.

It was a powerful hand.

T

Under the couch,
where the ground is littered
with the crumbs of past meals,
lost change that may never be found
and dust bunnies of startling size,
crouches *T*,
my fat, striped and fowl-tempered cat —
named after the Patron Saint of Hopeless Cases
(and a Polish poet).

While my wife,
pregnant both with child and ice cream,
dozes above him,
T glowers in his upholstered cave.
He passes his bristled tongue across one
crooked whisker.

He stretches out his right paw,
extending his pink-padded digits and revealing
his claws.

He squints out at the room with his one good eye.

On the radio, a nocturne plays to the fantasies of
my wife's dreams,
while *T* plots to steal our baby's breath.

The Man Who Spoke to Ghosts

The Man who Spoke to Ghosts went deaf,

at least that's what he told me
under the bridge
warmed by cheap wine
and Sterno flame.

You know you can't drink that shit to get high
anymore, right? he asked me.

He said it was great being deaf
because the whole world was wound up
neat and tight
in a package
in his head
where it hummed.
Now his ears were locks that kept it all in
and kept the voices out.

The Man who Spoke to Ghosts told me it was
nice to be alone,
for once,
with his red wine
and canned heat
and his own thoughts —
alone without the voices to bother him.

He said the ghosts were tedious and dull,
had no soul,
no life,
nothing interesting to say.

He said they bored the shit out of him
with their constant whining
and carping and pining
for the lives
they once had —
the lives they ignored when they had them.

He took another pull from his bottle,
gave me a slap on the knee,
and told me it was great being deaf.
Finally, a little peace, he said.

Above us the semis
and commuters
and joyriders
rumbled past,
shaking the concrete pillars of his home.
Of course the Man who Spoke to Ghosts heard
nothing.

I opened my mouth to say something
but stopped.
And the Man who Spoke to Ghosts went on
being deaf.

Bloody Fit Boys

The red-and-blues *wah-wah'ed* off the bar walls
as we all yelled for the jackal-headed jackoffs to
vacate the premises
posthaste.

The rabble roused and refused to go.
And the late night,
last call
standoff was underway.

The siren wail was lost in the
juke-box-bar-brawl braying.
It wasn't until I heard the screams that I knew
what was what.

The boy was young
and dressed like a girl
and uglied up
like homemade sin
lying outside,
face first,
having an intimate conversation
with cement.

The men and women in uniform looked bored
and put the boy-in-girls-clothes on a back board
and took statements
and whisked her away.

The fit young men,
with blood on their fists
in the new SUV,
were questioned
and cut loose.

The rabble relented and
wandered away,
and we returned to our work.

I got the letter a month later,
a summons to appear in court.

They asked me what I saw.

Nothing I said.

And that was that.
The bloody, fit boys
are probably still out there in their new SUV.

The boy in girls clothes is probably dead.

A Bird in Victoria Station

There is a bird in Victoria Station who will
never leave.

From her home in the bower of steel girders
she can watch the wandering travelers,
each a single shape, moving from somewhere
to somewhere —

all swarming past the snack vendors
and janitors,
the commuters
and backpackers,
the buskers
and bums.

Their voices lost
in the muddy squeal of the public address
speakers,
the constant screech of the trains
and the white-out white noise
of too many things all happening at once.

She will think the constant roar of humanity
is all the sound the world holds.
The bird will think the Earth is concrete
and tile,

and sprouts coffee kiosks
and dustbins
and hard metal benches.

She will never taste a worm or a grub.
She will think the Earth's bounty
is made of scraps of biscuits and scones.

The bird will think the world holds no
predators —

no cats or foxes or goshawks.
She will think she is at the apex of her food
chain,
the piece of muffin her prey.

The bird will think the sky is metal and glass,
that the limits of her world can be reached.
The Heavens attainable.

There is a bird in Victoria Station
who will grow fat
and happy
and die.

A Toast

Listen up, all —

This is a toast!

Here is to all of the lost children,
the wayward sons and daughters,
the abandoned and strays.

Here is to all of the cold cases
and lost causes,
the rejected and shamed.

So raise your glass, boys,
raise your glass.

To the ones who couldn't cut it
or the ones who didn't want to be cut.

Because this is our time.
It's not for the dead,
the forgotten,
the ghosts.

It's not for the shipwrecked
or wounded
or killed.

It's our time to be in *this* place,
our time to live.

But here is to all of the lost children,
the orphans,
the foundlings,
the waifs.
Here is to the ones who couldn't' make it,
the ones who didn't want to get made.

So here is to the lullabies
to all of the soft, small,
innocent things.

So raise your glass, boys,
raise your glass.

The Way Time Moves Across Asphalt in the Sand Hills of Nebraska

Time takes its time
across the blacktop.

It crosses the low scrub
and patchy dunes
at a pace of its own
determination.

Here Time has nothing but time on its hands,
so it moseys along the Western desert
and gladly yields right-of-way to fence posts
and cattle
and patches of musk thistle.

Time rests
on the center yellow line,
watching the asphalt stretch
from vanishing point
to vanishing point.

Time usually spends its time
ever-rushing forward,
hurtling onward,
rocketing us from the cradle to the grave.

Time flies, in other parts of the world,
but here, in the Sand Hills,
it takes its time.

It watches the lizards
and jackrabbits
and turkey vultures
zip past.

So while the sun waits to exit,
and the moon waits to enter
and I wait for my car to crest the next hill,

Time takes its time
and enjoys the view.

Tragic-Faced Woman

She is a tragic-faced woman,
a faded beauty,
a fallen homecoming queen.

She sings loud,
out loud,
all alone in a crowded bar
but the jukebox sets her free.

She is a tragic-faced woman —
always on the verge of tears,
always ready to cry.

But buy her another drink, boys,
buy another round
and she will tell you stories of her glory days;
she will tell you about her past.

She will spin tails of tragic triumphs,
of backyard, barbecue brawls and barroom
romance —
of near misses and the dearly missed.

She will tell you about loves
lost, traded and sometimes given away.

She will tell you that she has never met a man
she didn't like
or a cop she didn't hate.

She never left without a reason.
She never took the first swing,
and she never, ever backed down from a fight.

She raises her glass high and dares any man
in the room to kiss her
or fight her,
both will leave a mark.

Buy her another round boys and her eyes will
start to shine.
That hitch in her voice will fade and the edge of
tears will grow further away.

She will tell you about the time,
that time that she and her man . . .
not *that* man,
not her *last* man
but the one before . . .
about that time she and her man made it all the
way to Heber Springs, Arkansas
with five gallons in the tank and two cigarettes
between them.
Like Jesus unto his people,
Christ it was a miracle.

She is a tragic-faced woman,
a lost goddess,
a wandering warrior queen.

She holds court from her seat at the bar and
takes her tribute in pinball money
and Midori sours and propositions of dubious intent.

She will tell you about the days she spent, following
that band —
you know, the one with that song.
About how her eyes were opened,
how her life was changed forever,
at least for that summer.

Put another quarter in her jukebox, boys,
and she will tell you about her past,
she will tell you everything.

Except about her son.
But she sends him Christmas cards like
clockwork
and birthday cards in May.

She is a tragic-faced woman,
a faded beauty,
a fallen homecoming queen,
always just on the verge of tears.

But the bartender is still serving
and the house lights are still low,
and there are still a few songs we have yet to sing.

So step up boys,
who's going to buy the next round?

Winding Down

She was like a clock
winding down.

She tried to keep time
but that time
was running out.

She was like a clock
winding down
and all she could do
was watch
the hands
tick
slower.

Saturday Tragedies

Saturday tragedies make drunkards of us all.

They lie in wait,
lurking like junkies in doorways,
skulking like rapists in the alley.

They watch us from the tops of telephone poles,
through closet doors, opened just a crack,
and from behind boxes of Chex-Mix in the snack aisle.

Saturday tragedies are the worst of them all.

They'll hit you on Wednesday.
They'll hit you at Christmas.

They will bite you on dark November nights,
riding little needles of Winter wind.

They will sledgehammer you,
under the sun,
on the kinds of days that take away the sins
of the world.

Saturday tragedies make drunkards of us all
because when they hit us,
they never stop hitting.

It

It is like tracing the jagged geometry of your
teeth with your tongue,
like chasing a tickle down the spine
of a woman's back.

It is as sure as love,
as certain as death.
It is inevitable.

I have one waiting for me.
I can see It.
Hiding around the corners,
sneaking behind the edges,
slinking just beyond the frame.

It knows that I am there, waiting.
It waits for me to know that It is there.

It is always different.
Some days It wears a hat.
Some days It wears a wig.

Some days It ignores me altogether,
keeping still and pretending to be invisible.

Some days It gives a wink and a sly grin.

Weeks, sometimes months, can pass
where I never see It;

I only feel Its presence,
hovering just beyond my peripheral vision.

Years can go by where It is always, there,
a ubiquitous phantom,
always in my line of sight.

Sometimes It feels safe,
like an old lover,
or a dear aunt.

Once I swear I saw the flash and gleam of cruel steel,
just before It jerked its arm behind its back
and smiled.

We have a relationship,
It and I,

a grudging, unspoken friendship,
a mutual admiration society of distant admirers.

It walks me home from work.
I think It watches me sleep.
I swear that It once served me a drink.

There is one waiting for me
and some day I will find out what It is,
whether I like It or not.

A Change of Venue

I need a change of venue.
My emotional jury is biased.
My psychic press has already tried, convicted
and sentenced me.

How can I expect to get a fair trial,
here
where I committed —
where I *allegedly* committed my crimes.

That smoking gun wasn't mine.
I just picked it up.
No,
I don't know how my fingerprints got there.
I have a reasonable explanation for everything
and my alibis always dress in iron.

My confession?
Given under duress.
Hell it was given after they beat the heavenly
shit out of me.

And nobody will post my bond.
They say that I am a flight risk,
liable to leave my mental country at any time.

But it wasn't me!
I swear.

I will move for a continuance,
my witness list is incomplete,
hell it is nonexistent.

I am innocent, I swear.
Somebody engineered this
and left me hanging in the frame.

Somebody set me up to take the fall
and it is a long way down.

Besides, I am going to file for a mistrial
on the grounds that the judge is
an insufferable prick.

Weird New Sins

The world whirled past,
while we were busy,
perfecting weird
new sins,

while we were breaking in
the dust bins,
while we were busy,
picking at our
own
souls' scabs.

While we wasted away
the day
and loved every minute of it.

The World spun on
& on,
& we never knew.

The grass grew
& birds & flowers died.

And we didn't care.

The world spun on,
While we were perfecting,
weird, new sins.

Midnight Cafe

He's hearing voices in the Midnight café.
They're screaming loud, just a whisper in his
ear

and all the truckers drink their
coffee with their dying breath.

God knows they're just trying to make a buck.

Well, the lights are hydrogen bombs
and the benches, cold concrete,
and a butterfly scar spreads its wings across the
dawn of a waitress's cheek.

She must have let somebody's coffee get cold.

And the night-crawlers,
and midnight-runners and late-night prophets
of lost gods mingle over cracked cups
of interstellar black coffee,
and bear claws,

and laugh, while the Big Boys snarl past,
slashing open that old wound, I-80,
west-bound.

He's hearing voices in the Midnight Cafe,
he's receiving a message from the great-beyond,

a summons
from the heart of an imploded star,
or the belly of the earth,
or from somewhere deep beneath the hash browns
of his $4.99, blue plate special.

But there are flapjacks
and griddle cakes
and biscuits and gravy
and hot, open faced, roast beef sandwiches to be had.

So he settles back and sets the fillings in his
back teeth to the right frequency
and tunes in the tinfoil under his hat
(all for better reception)

and orders one more pot of La Brea sludge
from the girl with the boyish hips
and the swagger in her walk
and the deep, down home,
Georgia-peach drawl.

He's hearing voices,
he's receiving a message from up on high.

It's riding an open wavelength,
the frequency is clean.

The message is coming in loud and clear.

He is hearing voices
but they are definitely
telling him things that he should not hear.

Jackknife

He left her sleeping,
like a jackknife,
curled,
silent,
fetal.

He left her breathing slow and steady,
knees tucked into belly,
her body folded up for the night.

He left her to sit on her porch
and watch a hazy screen of clouds,
the color of a black and white movie,
scroll across the spotlight-moon,

to listen to the rustling night sounds
as a warm wind,
not due for another month,
is smuggled in on a low Santa Fe moan —

to listen to the chattering chirp of nighthawks
and watch the alley cats prowl their kingdoms,
slinking from shadow to shadow,
under the ghost-glow of light
from the second hand store's second story window.

He left her to breathe an even mix of
cigarette smoke and sharp night air.

To think.
To think long, random,
sometimes dirty thoughts,
amidst the chorus of distant police-cruiser wails
and the arias of car alarms.

He left her shining in the darkness,
a bright spot in the moonlight,
quiet and still.

He left her sleeping,
like a jackknife,
coiled,
latent,
final.

Fallen Empire

There is a fallen empire,
spread wide across the floor
of the living room
of your parents' home.

Forgotten, carpeted streets wind around
the spires of beer bottles, liquor bottles,
wine bottles,

wind around the temples of soup bowls,
lined with the remains of Lay's potato chips,
covered in chili sauce
and a squeeze of fresh lime.
A little trick that your mother picked up in Mexico.

An unearthed city built on bricks of empty
cigarette packs,
decaying ziggurats of heaping ashtrays,
a foundation of stale cigarette smoke,

a ruined Xanadu of refuse,
nestled among mountains made of living room
furniture.

And you and I, lying on the couch,
catching up after all these years,
lying among the ancient relics of a long dead people.

You tell me that your life is good,
your boyfriend is kind
and you just love your new job.

And the clock slowly ticks down the eons as the
kingdom around us,
sinks even deeper into the sands of time.

But you are just home for the holidays,
and your folks have been asleep for hours,
and, Christ, it's been since high school.

So we chat,
lying next to each other,
like we did,
an age ago.

We idly waste time,
and breath,
and lives.

We are the founders of this lost and abandoned city,
and we don't seem to care.

We are the gods and creators of this
ancient civilization.
We are the excavators of its
archaeological remains

but we have other things on our minds.

So we cycle through the, *I-am-so-glad-that-
you-are-happy's*
and the *good-for-you's*.

And the lost city of a once-proud people,
crumbles around us under the weight of age.

And,
without warning,
I feel you press
my fingers

into you,
under the blanket,
under your skirt.

And the pyramids that we made
continue crumbling.

But your hot, summer-monsoon wind on my neck,
your hand, firm and insistent,
that look in your eyes that I still remember.

And for a moment.

But we must have respect for this sunken city,
this snapshot of a civilization,
snuffed out like Pompeii,
buried under an avalanche of ash
and time.

We must have respect for the dead.

Direct Orders to the Things That Live in My Head

All right,
listen up.

All of you hairy, spiny things,
you slimy, segmented gut-gnawing worms.
All of you black, chitinous crawlers,
you howlers,
you screechers,
you mad-man mumblers.

Listen up
and listen good.
This shit has got to stop.

This ain't no democracy,
no part-time job
where you can sit on your ass
and get high in the walk-in cooler.

This here is *indentured sevitude.*
Slavery, plain and simple,
a chain gang
and I own your sorry asses.
Got it?

Now, I am tired of you
getting up
in the middle of the night
and keeping me awake.

Well I am tired, man,
I am tired of you crawling around,
clawing at the walls of my skull
at all god-forsaken hours.

And you,

yes you,

the one that looks like a little, black
fluffy kitten, and just last night
told me, that my mamma's goin' to Hell.
That ain't cool.

So no more.
No more Mr. Kind Boss.
No more Mr. Nice Boss.

It's time for Mr. Hard Boss,
I'm talking Mr. Walkin' Boss.
with a rifle and a cane,
and a sap,
just to make sure that there are
no more little communication failures.

So it's a set of leg-irons for all.
And the next one of you
caught, creeping in the hallways of my dreams
and I am starving you all.

That's right.
You get no more painful memories,
no more banquets lined with bad regrets, lost
loves
and sweet lovin' booze.

No more broken glass
and razor wire
and good intentions gone sour.

So listen up,
all you motherless sons,
all you bat-winged bastards,
you scorpion-tailed children of my psyche.

Stay in your boxes when the lights are off.

And if you can't stay in your coffins
and shoe boxes,
and sock drawers,
and let me sleep,

then I'm gonna' stop drinking.

That's right.

No more bad decisions,
no more I-wish-I-had
or I-wish-I-hadn'ts.

I'm going to cop to my crimes.
I'm going to call back,
and I'm gonna' spend more time.
I'm going to work harder.

I'm gonna' straighten up and fly right.

And if you don't let me sleep, well hell,
I might even go to church.

A Poem Named Steve

I met a poem once,
his name was Steve.
He was half free-verse,
half ode,
on his mother's side.

He asked me if I would join him for coffee.

We took a booth in the back of a little diner and
ordered a
pot of coal-black coffee.

When the waitress deposited the pot and cups
on our table,
Steve pulled a little, silver flask from somewhere
within his rumpled grey suit jacket
and discreetly tipped a three-count
of its contents into his cup.

It smelled strong and sweet,
a bit like amaretto.
He waggled the flask in my direction
as an offering.
I declined.

We talked.
We talked about life and all of the
niggling little
details attached to it.

We talked about loss and
love and all of the spurious,
random things
that bless
and damn us
in the end.

Steve kept tipping the silver flask
into his coffee mug,
glancing
guiltily over his shoulder,
as if he was waiting to be caught.

He told me about his life,
pining about his losses,
crowing over his victories.

I smiled and nodded,
squeezing a few words in,
slightly edgewise.

We kept ordering
pot
after
pot of tar-black coffee
and Steve's flask never went dry.

Finally I asked him what was in it.
He said it was the poem's little secret —
Inspiration.

He was beginning to list a little in his seat.
He was rocking gently, back and forth,
like he was on a ship adrift at sea,
and he was starting to slur his words.

Finally, Steve leaned over the table
and winked at me, conspiratorially.

He said, *We are all liars and thieves.*

I asked him what he meant
but he suddenly sat bolt upright
and cast a glance around him,
like a felon smelling police dogs on his trail.

He muttered something about
being caught short just at the moment
and I told him that I'd pick up the check.
Without another word he hurried from the diner
and out into the street.

I saw that he had left the little, chrome flask
sitting on the table.
I couldn't help myself.
I snatched it up
and took a long pull from it.

It was strong and sweet, a bit like amaretto.

Everything that I have just told you was a lie,
stolen from someone else.

The Road

The road was carcass
after carcass
— coyote,
cat,
possum,
dog —
all flying past at speed.

A non-stop, high-speed chase scene.

The road didn't want you to stop
and you couldn't.

It pulled you onward,
yanked you forward,
jerked you over the center-line.

The road was carcass after carcass,
body after body
but
the road was a ribbon
that wound around
the package of the earth.

The road made the world a gift.

The road was just a track in the sands of time;
it was the temporary reminder of the inevitable.

The road was a cursive we carved into our world,
a totem,
a sign we made for the future.

It shaped the landscape
and cut the storm clouds in half.

It cracked and buckled and
— reluctantly —
let the weeds
peek through
the jagged gaps.

The road was our hope
and promise.

We knew it would outlive us.

It carried us away
and stayed behind to watch
the towers crumble.

It gave its life for ours.

The road did its job.

The Ghosts Checked Out

They told me the old hotel was haunted,
but it wasn't.

They all left
when the contractors and corporate bosses and
consultants moved in.

The kid with the greasy hair packed it in —
said he was fed up with this whole specter-game
— said he was going to beg for his old job back,
back down at the boneyard.

The old lady who rode the elevators,
all night, every night?
Turned in her union card
and quit.

All of the ghosts checked out of the old hotel.
They left no forwarding addresses,
no contact info.
They didn't fill out a single comment card.

My friend on the other side told me the ghosts split.

They pulled stakes when their lovely lounge
became a big-screen, sports-scene,
margaritas and appetizers,
after-work-friendly bar.

The ghosts checked out and now
the old hotel is empty,
no matter what the guest registry says.

The boy? Back to his grave.

The old lady? Wandering the halls of her old
old-folks home

And the couple who used to dance in the night
(he in a tux and she in a gown, a Nick and Nora
Charles of the afterlife)?
Checked out.

But maybe,
maybe they spend their nights
in the shiny new nightclub
just opened on the corner.
Or maybe they sit at the tables of the
restaurant that moved into the carcass
of the old pharmacy.

Or,
more likely,
they still dance
and sip rye Manhattans and sloe gin fizzes
in the speakeasy basement
of the old movie house
just up the street.

Thaddeus Haverkamp was raised in Kearney, Nebraska where he received (somehow) his B.A. in English literature. He moved to Lawrence, Kansas in 1995 with the intention of housesitting for one summer. So, mostly through inaction, he has made Northeastern Kansas his permanent home.

d in the USA
information can be obtained
Gtesting.com
)508310823
LV00005B/900